NOTE TO PARENTS

Welcome to Kingfisher Readers! This program is designed to help young readers build skills, confidence, and a love of reading as they explore their favorite topics.

These tips can help you get more from the experience of reading books together. But remember, the most important thing is to make reading fun!

Tips to Warm Up Before Reading

- Look through the book with your child. Ask them what they notice about the pictures.
- Wonder aloud together. Ask questions and make predictions. What will this book be about? What are some words we could expect to find on these pages?

While Reading

- Take turns or read together until your child takes over.
- Point to the words as you say them.
- When your child gets stuck on a word, ask if the picture could help. Then think about the first letter too.
- Accept and praise your child's contributions.

After Reading

- Look back at the things your child found interesting. Encourage connections to other things you both know.
- Draw pictures or make models to explore these ideas.
- Read the book again soon, to build fluency.

With five distinct levels and a wealth of appealing topics, the Kingfisher Readers series provides children with an exciting way to learn to read about the world around them. Enjoy!

Ellie Costa, M.S. Ed.
Literacy Specialist, Bank Street School for Children, New York

KINGFISHER READERS

level 3

Vikings

Philip Steele

KINGFISHER
NEW YORK

KINGFISHER
LONDON & NEW YORK

Copyright © Kingfisher 2014
Published in the United States by Kingfisher,
175 Fifth Ave., New York, NY 10010
Kingfisher is an imprint of Macmillan Children's Books, London.
All rights reserved.

Distributed in the U.S. and Canada by Macmillan,
175 Fifth Ave., New York, NY 10010

Library of Congress Cataloging-in-Publication data
has been applied for.

Series editor: Thea Feldman
Literacy consultant: Ellie Costa, Bank Street School for Children, New York

ISBN: 978-0-7534-7148-7 (HB)
ISBN: 978-0-7534-7149-4 (PB)

Kingfisher books are available for special promotions
and premiums. For details contact: Special Markets
Department, Macmillan, 175 Fifth Ave., New York, NY 10010.

For more information, please visit
www.kingfisherbooks.com

Printed in China
9 8 7 6 5 4 3 2 1
1TR/0314/WKT/UG/105MA

Picture credits
The Publisher would like to thank the following for permission to reproduce their
material. Every care has been taken to trace copyright holders. However, if there
have been unintentional omissions or failure to trace copyright holders, we apologize
and will, if informed, endeavor to make corrections in any future edition.
Top = t; Bottom = b; Center = c; Left = l; Right = r
Cover Kingfisher; Pages 7 Peter Kuiper/Wikipedia;
9t Corbis/Werner Forman Archive; 9b Shutterstock/Kristina Postnikova; 12 Shutterstock/Mircea
Bezergheanu; 15t Art Archive/ Oldsaksammlung, Oslo/Dagli Orti; 15b Corbis/Werner Forman Archive;
17 Corbis/Werner Forman Archive; 19 Corbis/Werner Forman Archive; 20 Alamy/Troy GB Images;
23 Corbis/Ted Spiegel; 26 Corbis/Ted Spiegel; 28 Art Archive/ Musee de la Tapisserie/Gianni Dagli Orti;
all other illustrations from the Kingfisher archive.

Contents

Who were the Vikings?

Norway, Sweden, and Denmark are countries in the north of Europe. The lands there have lakes, mountains, big forests, and rocky coasts. The winters are cold and snowy, but the summers are warm.

The people who lived on these lands between 750 and 1100 CE are known as Vikings. The name Viking means "sea **raider**." Vikings traveled the seas and attacked other people. But they were also farmers, fishermen, and **traders**.

There are many stories called sagas written about Vikings. They tell us how Vikings lived long ago.

Viking tales
At Viking gatherings, poets called skalds told exciting tales about battles, ships, treasures, and monsters.

Vikings at sea and home

Vikings traveled far and wide. They raided towns and villages. They seized gold from churches, burned buildings, and stole cattle. They killed people or carried them off to become slaves.

Vikings were not just raiders. They also cleared forests, built towns, farmed the land, and fished.

There were many successful Viking traders, as well as expert craft workers. Viking settlers passed laws too.

Viking writing

The Vikings spoke a language we call Old Norse. It was sometimes written down in letters called runes. You can see runes on this stone.

Gods and giants

Vikings believed in many gods. Odin was
the father of the gods. People believed that
he rode an eight-legged horse. On stormy
nights, they thought they could see Odin
galloping across the sky. Odin had two
pet **ravens**. They flew around the world
every day and told him what they saw.

God of thunder

This is a carving of Thor, who was the god of thunder and lightning. He had a big hammer, which he used to fight giants and monsters.

Vikings believed in other worlds too, where there were giants, monsters, snakes, and spirits. At the center of the **universe** was a gigantic ash tree, named Yggdrasil (say IG-druh-sil).

The way to the gods

Vikings believed that the world of humans was connected to the world of the gods by a great rainbow bridge.

In the longhouse

Many Vikings lived in farming **settlements** with stables and barns. The biggest building was the longhouse. It was a long wooden hut with a **thatched** roof.

Inside, it was dark and smoky. A fire burned for warmth, and the floor was covered in dried grass. Raised platforms along the walls were used as beds or seats. Families, farm workers, and slaves all slept here.

Women prepared
ood and wove
loth on a loom.
Men repaired
shing lines, tools,
nd weapons.

Games and dice
On winter nights,
Vikings sat by the
fire and played
dice or board
games such
as chess.

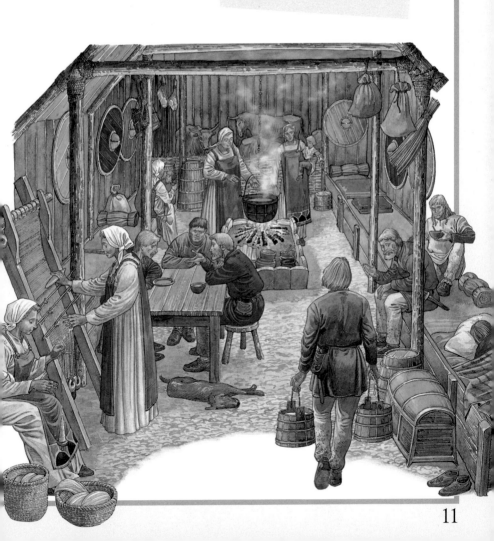

Farming and food

Viking farmers grew wheat, barley, rye, peas, and cabbages. They raised geese, sheep, goats, pigs, horses, and cattle. They got eggs, milk, meat, wool, and leather from the animals.

The Vikings also hunted wild birds, reindeer, and wild **boar**. The seas were full of fish, such as cod and herring, which they caught in nets.

Farmers raised goats for meat and milk.

Drinking horns
The Vikings drank wine, beer, or mead from hollow cattle horns. Mead was a strong drink made from honey.

...eople often salted or dried meat and fish ...o it would keep longer. They cooked over a ...re or stewed food in **cauldrons**.

Making beautiful things

Viking women wove thread into cloth to make clothes and blankets. They wore simple, long dresses with long **tunics** over them. The shoulder straps were fastened with beautiful pins and chains. Men wore long **breeches** and woollen tunics.

Vikings made jewelry from gold, silver, and colored stone

iking craftsmen
urved horns,
alrus tusks,
ood, and stones.

This wood carving
shows a Viking
making a sword.

**Pictures and
patterns**
Viking designs
had swirling
patterns and
included
birds, snakes,
and monsters.

Towns and trade

Most towns
were built by rivers or
harbors, since most travel
took place on the water. There were
few good roads.

Houses and workshops were made
of wood. People dug ditches or built
fences around the towns to prevent
enemy attacks.

...eople bought
...ood, tools,
...ots and pans,
...nd jewelry in
...wn markets.
...ilks, furs, and
...pices from
...araway places
...ere for
...le too.

Viking money
At first, Vikings did
not have their own
coins. So people
just traded things at
the market.

Off to war

Vikings built many types of boats. They had little rowing boats and sturdy ships that carried heavy **cargo**. Their finest ships, called **longships**, were used for crossing the oceans or going to war.

Viking longships were designed to be fast. Each ship was rowed by a crew of 30 or more men. Every man had one oar. The ship had a square sail made of wool or linen.

All the sailors were also fighters, and they were heavily armed. Shields were hung along the sides of the ship to protect the rowers from enemy arrows.

Dragon ships
A longship had a high wooden **prow**. It was often carved into a snarling dragon shape.

Warriors and weapons

Most Vikings were farmers and fishermen who joined their **jarl** for raids.

They wore everyday clothes into battle, as well as a helmet made of leather or iron.
A jarl often wore something called a mail shirt that was made from iron rings.

ikings fought
ith iron swords,
pears, axes, and
ows and arrows.
heir big, round
hields were made
f wood, with
n iron knob in
he middle.

Berserk!

Some warriors worked themselves into a fury before a battle. They were called "berserkir," and they wore shirts of bear skin. Today we still use the word "berserk" to mean crazy.

Raiders and settlers

Viking raiders wanted to be rich and powerful. They attacked villages, towns, and big cities. They attacked Great Britain, Ireland, Germany, France, and Spain.

The Vikings set up winter camps in foreign lands. Then they built new settlements overseas and took control of whole regions.

The Vikings took over York in England. In France, they took over a large area of land called Normandy.

Archaeologists find Viking remains under the streets of Dublin, in Ireland.

Nicknames
Viking warriors had scary nicknames, such as Erik Bloodaxe and Thorfinn Skull-Splitter.

Sailing west

The Vikings sailed west across the oceans.
Between 874 and 930 CE, they settled in
Iceland. There were few trees, so they built
longhouses from stone, grass, and earth.
Wherever they settled, they set up **assemblie**
to make laws and solve arguments.

Sometimes storms
blew Viking longships
even further west and
the sailors sighted
unknown lands

Viking
assemblie
were held i
the open ai

24

Viking settlers hunted walrus and seals off the icy coasts of Greenland.

n 982 CE, Erik the Red led settlers to an icy
nd. He called it Greenland, hoping that
is name would attract more people.

rik's son was Leif the Lucky. In about
002 CE, he sailed down the coast of
orthern North America. The Vikings

tried to settle in
North America,
but they were
fiercely attacked
by the Native
Americans.

Burials and burnings

Vikings returned from their travels with a lot of treasure. In times of war or trouble, they buried the treasure to keep it safe. People are still discovering these Viking treasures.

Viking treasure found in Sweden

In the hall of Odin
Vikings believed that warriors who died in battle met the god Odin. They feasted forever in his great hall, Valholl.

Archaeologists also find treasure in places where Vikings were buried. Some dead Viking chiefs were put on their ships, which were then set on fire. Others were placed inside ships and buried beneath mounds of earth.

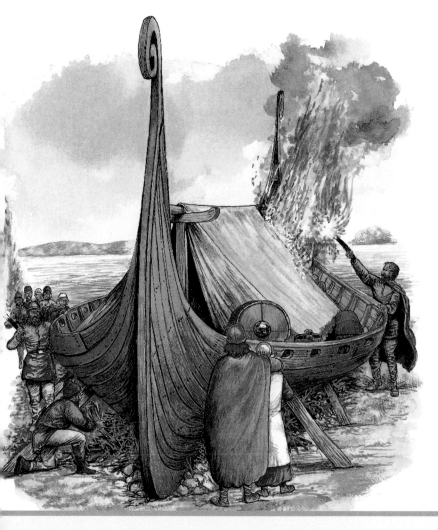

The end of an age

After about 960 CE, many Vikings became Christians. For years, people wore the hammer symbol of the god Thor alongside the cross of Christianity. By the 1080s, all the Viking lands were Christian. The Vikings became part of larger kingdoms, and they stopped raiding.

When the Normans invaded England in 1066 their boats looked just like Viking longships.

Descendants of the Vikings who settled in France, called Normans, conquered large parts of Europe, from England to Italy. The old Viking lands make up the modern countries of Denmark, Sweden, Norway, and Iceland.

VIKING DATES

789 CE	Vikings start to raid the British Isles.
841	Vikings are based in Dublin, Ireland.
867	Vikings capture York, England.
874	Vikings settle Iceland.
911	Vikings win Normandy, in France.
960	Christianity starts in Viking lands.
982	Erik the Red reaches Greenland.
1002	Leif the Lucky explores northern North America.
c.1100	The Viking age comes to an end.

Glossary

archaeologist someone who digs up and studies ancient ruins and remains

assembly a group of people who make laws and important decisions

boar a wild pig

breeches a type of pants

cargo goods loaded on a ship

cauldron a big, metal cooking pot

descendant a relative of a person who lived a long time ago

harbor a place where ships stay and are prepared for their journeys

jarl a Viking chief or nobleman

longship a long, narrow ship with oars and a single sail

prow the front of a ship

ider someone who attacks others and steals
om them

ven a big, black bird in the crow family

ttlements an area where people build places
live and work that had no such places before

atched covered with straw or reeds

ader a person who buys and sells goods

nic a long, loose garment that is usually worn
er other clothing

niverse everything that exists, including
ter space

Index

If you have enjoyed reading
this book, look out for more in
the Kingfisher Readers series!

**Collect
and read
them all!**

KINGFISHER READERS: LEVEL 3

Ancient Rome ☐
Cars ☐
Creepy Crawlies ☐
Dinosaur World ☐
Firefighters ☐
Record Breakers—The Biggest ☐
Vikings ☐
Volcanoes ☐

KINGFISHER READERS: LEVEL 4

The Arctic and Antarctica ☐
Flight ☐
Human Body ☐
Pirates ☐
Rivers ☐
Sharks ☐
Spiders—Deadly Predators ☐
Weather ☐

For a full list of Kingfisher Readers books, plus
guidance for teachers and parents and activities
and fun stuff for kids, go to the Kingfisher Readers
website: **www.kingfisherreaders.com**